TRIBES of NATIVE AMERICA

Nez Perce

edited by Marla Felkins Ryan
and Linda Schmittroth

BLACKBIRCH
PRESS

THOMSON
★
GALE

San Diego • Detroit • New York • San Francisco • Cleveland
New Haven, Conn. • Waterville, Maine • London • Munich

Photo credits: Cover Courtesy of Northwestern University Library; cover © National Archives; cover © Photospin; cover © Perry Jasper Photography; cover © Picturequest; cover © Seattle Post-Intelligencer Collection, Museum of History & Industry; cover © Blackbirch Press Archives; cover © Library of Congress; cover © PhotoDisc; pages 5, 6, 7, 9, 17 © CORBIS; pages 3, 8, 12, 14, 18, 19, 20, 22, 27, 29 © nativestock.com; page 9 © Greenhaven Picture Archive; page 10 © Washington State Historical Society; page 11 © Hulton Archive; page 13 © Oregon Historical Society; page 16, 21 © Northwestern University Library; pages 24-25 © Northwest Museum of Arts & Culture/Eastern Washington State Historical Society, Spokane, Washington; page 26 © National Park Service, Nez Perce National Historical Park, National Park Service Collection; pages 30, 31 © AP Wide World

LIBRARY OF CONGRESS CATALOGING-IN-PUBLICATION DATA

Nez Perce / Marla Felkins Ryan, book editor; Linda Schmittroth, book editor.
   v. cm. — (Tribes of Native America)
Includes bibliographical references and index. Contents: Name — Religion — Language — Economy — Daily life — Arts.
   ISBN 1-56711-616-7 (hardback : alk. paper)
   1. Nez Perce Indians—Juvenile literature. [1. Nez Perce Indians. 2. Indians of North America—Northwest, Pacific.] I. Ryan, Marla Felkins. II. Schmittroth, Linda. III. Series.
   E99.N5 N47 2003
   979.5004'9741—dc21
                                                        2002007855

Table of Contents

NEZ PERCE

Name

Nez Perce (pronounced nez *PURSE*; also spelled Nez Percé and pronounced *nay per-SAY*). The Nez Perce called themselves *Nee-Me-Poo* or *Nimipu,* which meant "our people." The name *Nez Perce* means "pierced nose" in French. The name was first used by early fur traders, even though the tribe did not traditionally practice nose piercing.

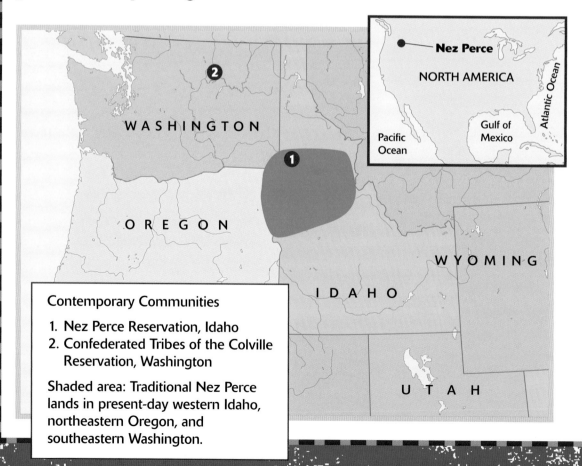

Nez Perce

NORTH AMERICA

Pacific Ocean

Gulf of Mexico

Atlantic Ocean

WASHINGTON

OREGON

IDAHO

WYOMING

UTAH

Contemporary Communities

1. Nez Perce Reservation, Idaho
2. Confederated Tribes of the Colville Reservation, Washington

Shaded area: Traditional Nez Perce lands in present-day western Idaho, northeastern Oregon, and southeastern Washington.

Today, most descendants of the Nez Perce tribe live in Idaho and Washington.

Location

The Nez Perce lived on lands in present-day western Idaho, northeastern Oregon, and southeastern Washington. Today, most of the descendants of the tribe live on the Nez Perce Reservation near Lapwai, Idaho, or on the Colville Reservation in the state of Washington.

Population

There were approximately 6,000 Nez Perce in 1800; there were 1,500 in 1900. In a 1990 population count by the U.S. Bureau of the Census, 4,003 people identified themselves as members of the Nez Perce tribe.

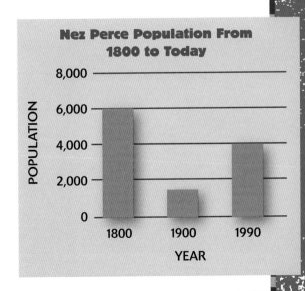

Nez Perce Population From 1800 to Today

Origins and group affiliations

Before the Europeans came, the Nez Perce had lived for hundreds of years in small villages along the Clearwater, Salmon, and Snake Rivers in the Pacific Northwest. They are linked to other tribes in that region, including the Yakima, Umatilla, Klickitat, and Walla Walla.

The Nez Perce fished in nearby rivers. They often lived in small villages along rivers in the Pacific Northwest.

The Nez Perce were once the most powerful tribe in the Northwest.

Once, the Nez Perce were one of the largest and most powerful tribes of the Northwest. They controlled a large piece of land along the Clearwater and Snake Rivers in what is now Idaho. They also had lands in Oregon and Washington. They lived as semi-wandering fishermen, hunters, and gatherers.

HISTORY

Horses bring changes

Before the Nez Perce acquired horses in the early 1700s, they fished, hunted on foot, or gathered wild plants for food. The use of horses soon changed their lifestyle. They started to trade with nearby tribes and began to take yearly trips to the Great Plains to hunt buffalo. Their rich grasslands let the Nez Perce raise larger herds of horses than many other tribes. They became skilled horse breeders and trainers. They had great success with the sturdy, spotted horses now called Appaloosas.

Appaloosas made trade with other tribes possible.

Lewis and Clark were taken in and fed by Nez Perce tribe members in 1805.

The Nez Perce had good relations with most nearby tribes, except those to the south, such as the Shoshone, Northern Paiute, and Bannock. Every summer, though, the Nez Perce traded peacefully with their enemies at a large gathering.

Whites move to tribal lands

The first contact between the Nez Perce and non-native people took place in 1805. At that time, the Lewis and Clark expedition wandered into the Wallowa Valley in western Idaho. The American explorers were cold, tired, and had little food left. The Nez Perce helped the members of the expedition and may have saved them from

1869
Transcontinential Railroad is completed

1877
During the Nez Perce War, Chief Joseph and his people try to flee to Canada. They are chased by U.S. army troops and overcome.

1917–1918
WWI fought in Europe

1929
Stock market crash begins the Great Depression

1941
Bombing at Pearl Harbor forces United States into WWII

1945
WWII ends

1950s
Reservations no longer controlled by federal government

1996
The Nez Perce are invited back to the Wallowa Valley

starvation. Later, the Nez Perce helped Meriwether Lewis and William Clark build boats, and guided the explorers to the Pacific Coast. Over the next few decades, the Nez Perce began to have friendly relations with French-Canadian and American fur traders, missionaries, and settlers.

Through the mid-1800s, the number of white settlers in the Northwest greatly increased. For the most part, the Nez Perce stayed out of the conflicts that hurt other tribes. They signed the Walla Walla Council of 1855. This treaty gave some of their ancestral land to the government. In exchange, the Nez Perce received money and a guarantee that the rest of their lands—13 million acres—would be left alone. Soon after, the governor of Washington

The Walla Walla Council of 1855 sits down to dinner.

Territory, Isaac Ingalls Stevens, wrote a letter to an eastern newspaper. In the letter, Stevens said that the Northwest was open for white settlement. Several area tribes were angry and reacted with violence. The Nez Perce, however, stayed neutral. They did not take part in the wars waged by other tribes against the United States.

In the early 1860s, gold was found on Nez Perce lands. Fortune seekers chose to ignore the 1855 treaty. In 1863, Nez Perce leaders tried but failed to reach a new treaty agreement. Stevens then got the signatures of a few members of the tribe on a document that gave away another 7 million acres of Nez Perce land. This document came to be known as the Thief Treaty. It cost the Nez Perce their claim to Wallowa Valley. Despite their anger, the Nez Perce were still peaceful in their relations with whites. They showed that they were unhappy, however, when they failed to go along with the treaty.

Nez Perce leader, Young Chief Joseph

Nez Perce surrender

When Nez Perce leader Old Chief Joseph died in 1871, his son Young Chief Joseph became the head of the Wallowa group. In 1876, he met with U.S.

government officials. He told them that he would not honor the 1863 Thief Treaty and give up the tribe's ancestral valley. The government did not listen. The tribe was given 30 days to leave Wallowa Valley and move to a reservation near Lapwai, Idaho. When Chief Joseph realized that the only way not to move was to go to war, he agreed to leave. He said sadly, "I would give up everything rather than have the blood of my people on my hands."

Before the move began, young rebels from the tribe attacked a group of whites. They killed three men and wounded another. Chief Joseph, along with 250 men, 500 women, children, and elderly members of the tribe reluctantly joined the rebels as they fled the valley. They hoped to find safety in Canada. Nearly 2,000 U.S. army troops set out to chase them. This began the Nez Perce War of 1877.

The final battle in the Nez Perce War of 1877.

THE BATTLE — ADVANCE OF THE SKIRMIS

END OF THE NEZ PERCÉS WAR—SURRENDER OF CHIEF JOSEPH.—From Sketches in the Field.—[See Page 906.]

Over the next four months, the Nez Perce traveled 1,600 miles. They crossed Idaho, Wyoming, and Montana. They traveled over mountains, through canyons, and across rivers. In all, they fought 14 battles against the better-equipped U.S. army. Until the last battle, they were able to outsmart and outfight the larger force.

Chief Joseph delivers his famous surrender speech.

Their final battle took place just 30 miles from the Canadian border. It lasted for six days. The Nez Perce fought off one army unit but were finally surrounded by another. Chief Joseph then gave his famous surrender speech: "I am tired. My heart is sick and sad. From where the Sun now stands, I will fight no more forever."

The Clearwater, Idaho, Nez Perce Indian Reservation

Sent to reservations

After their surrender, the Nez Perce were sent to reservations in Kansas and Oklahoma. They ended up on the Colville Reservation near Nespelem, Washington. Part of the tribe was placed on the Nez Perce Reservation near Lapwai, Idaho. The Nez Perce refused to let the U.S. government reorganize them. Instead, in 1948, they set up their own tribal constitution.

Religion

The Nez Perce felt a deep spiritual tie to the earth. They lived in harmony with nature. For the Nez Perce, all living things were closely related to each other and to people. Each member of the tribe had a guardian spirit, or *wyakin,* that protected him or her from harm and gave help when needed. The Nez Perce often carried small bundles of materials that represented their wyakins.

Many modern Nez Perce have adopted Christianity but they combine it with elements of the Dreamer religion. The Dreamer religion is a traditional Nez Perce faith. People who practice this religion believe that in past times, their leaders had special dreams. These dreams predicted important events.

Government

Before they met white missionaries in the 1840s, the Nez Perce's 70 small communities did not have a formal system of government. Each village had a council of three or four respected men. One of these men was called chief. In general, the job went to the person who had the most relatives in the village. When a chief died, his son usually took his place. The chief resolved disputes and disciplined unruly children.

The Nez Perce had few laws. Social pressure kept order. Meetings to discuss problems took place when people gathered to fish or harvest crops. Even then, no tribe member had to obey any group decision.

Each independent village or group had a headman who spoke for his own people. When a major decision needed to be made, the headmen and other respected people met in a tribal council to try to reach an agreement.

In the 1990s, the Nez Perce Tribal Executive Committee was made up of elected officers who served three-year terms. The committee managed many different tribal affairs.

A Nez Perce tribe member carries fish in a mesh bag.

Economy

Before white people moved to their lands, the Nez Perce dug roots, picked berries, and hunted small animals for food. Every May and June, they caught salmon. They dried and preserved the fish to eat throughout the year.

The people rarely went far from their homes. The horses that the Nez Perce acquired in the 1700s soon became valuable for trade and for

Law enforcement is just one type of job available on Nez Perce Reservation.

traveling long distances. Horses also helped the Nez Perce hunt buffalo. The Nez Perce traded dried berries and dried cakes made of sweet-tasting camas lily bulbs. They also traded corn-like roots called kouse, as well as salmon oil and dried salmon. They traded the horns from mountain sheep, bowls, cedar-root baskets, eagle feathers, and hunting tools.

Some modern Nez Perce farm and work with lumber. Others have jobs in medicine, law, engineering, and many other fields. The tribe also farms nearly 38,000 acres of reservation land. Wheat is the main crop. Other crops include barley, dry peas, lentils, canola, bluegrass seed, alfalfa, and hay. Cattle are also raised.

DAILY LIFE

Families

Nez Perce had large families. Women and men had different jobs within the family.

The Nez Perce often had large families. It was mainly the mother's job to raise children, but the task was shared by uncles, aunts, cousins, and older siblings. Men and women did different jobs in a family. Women picked berries, dug up camas bulbs, and made pottery. Men hunted and fished.

Buildings

For hundreds of years, the Nez Perce lived in houses covered with plant material. In the summer, when they moved in search of food, they lived in quickly built lean-tos. These were made of a pole framework covered with woven mats of plant fibers. The Nez Perce's winter shelters were pole-framed structures covered with layers of cedar bark, sagebrush, packed grass, and earth. Each winter dwelling had a small door and a smoke hole in the roof. Several families usually lived in each house, and there were five to six houses in a village.

Several Nez Perce families often lived in one large house.

After the Nez Perce made contact with other tribes, they decorated their clothes with beads and elk's teeth.

As horses came into wider use, the tribe could move around more and was able to meet other tribes. After these encounters, the Nez Perce built structures that were larger and more complex. Winter houses sometimes reached 100 feet in length and housed many families. Hide-covered tepees were used during the summer, when the Nez Perce traveled to hunt and fish.

Clothing

In early times, shredded cedar bark, deerskin, or rabbitskin were used to make clothing. In summer, men usually wore capes and breechcloths (flaps of material that cover the front and back and hang from the waist). They added fur robes and leggings when it got cold. Nez Perce women were known for the large basket hats they wove out of dried leaves and plant fibers. Men wore their hair in a high mound that stood straight up from the forehead. The rest of the hair was braided, and it hung down over the chest.

By the early 1800s, the Nez Perce had made contact with other tribes of the Pacific Coast and Great Plains. They soon began to decorate their clothing with shells, elk teeth, and beads, as the other tribes did. Women began to wear long dresses of buckskin with fringe at the hem and sleeves.

Food

It was a very time-consuming task for the Nez Perce to gather food. They lived in dry, rugged, high country. The people fished, hunted, and gathered

Nez Perce men speared fish for food for their families.

fruit and vegetables from spring through fall. They stored any extra food for winter use. In the spring, they fished for the large numbers of salmon that swam upstream. To fish, the Nez Perce used spears, hand-held and weighted nets, and small brush traps.

Although hunting was often difficult in their homeland, the Nez Perce managed to hunt elk, deer, and mountain sheep with bows and arrows. To get near their prey and kill them more easily,

Tools used for hunting and gathering

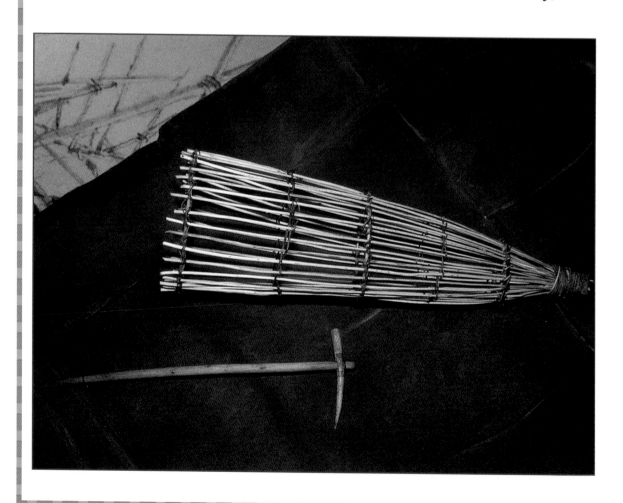

the Nez Perce sometimes disguised themselves in animal furs or worked as a group to surround an animal herd. After they started to use horses, the Nez Perce sent a party to the Great Plains each year to hunt buffaloes.

In the spring, Nez Perce women went to the hillsides and used sharp sticks to dig up kouse (roots). The kouse was ground up and boiled to make soup, or was shaped into cakes and dried for later use. Other plants were gathered in summer. Among them were wild onions and carrots, bitterroots, blackberries, strawberries, huckleberries, and nuts. In late summer, several Nez Perce bands came together to gather camas bulbs. These bulbs were often steamed and then made into a dough or gruel (a kind of a thin, watery soup).

Education

Grandparents provided much of a child's education. From them, girls learned how to gather food and run a household. Boys learned how to hunt and fish with small bows and arrows. Children also learned rules of social conduct, as well as tribal history, from their grandparents.

This tradition continues today. Tribal elders teach children at Nez Perce summer camps how important it is to preserve their culture.

Grandparents were Nez Perce children's primary teachers.

Healing practices

Nez Perce doctors, called shamans (pronounced *SHAH-munz* or *SHAY-munz*), could be male or female. Shamans were believed to have miraculous powers. They could

change the weather or cause evil people to have bad
luck. Shamans could even cure the sick with sacred
songs and herbal remedies. Sometimes, the shamans
held ceremonies to purify spirits before special
events, or to cure illness.

Men and women wear outfits decorated with feathers and beads to traditional dances.

Dances

Today, both adults and children are encouraged to perform traditional Nez Perce dances to the beat of a drum. During men's traditional dances, the dancers move to a drumbeat and look down as though to examine the tracks of wild game or the enemy. In the Men's Fancy Dance, they wear outfits adorned with feathers and ribbons. These dancers perform fast, spinning movements to a quick beat. During the Grass Dance, they use a graceful, swaying motion that looks like prairie grass as it bends in the wind. In their traditional dance, women wear beautiful dresses decorated with beadwork, porcupine quills, elk's teeth, and ribbons. They gently bounce, dip, and sway to the slow beat of a drum. During the Jingle Dance, they move in dresses adorned with cones made from the lids of metal cans.

Oral literature

Nez Perce families often gathered to tell stories, especially during the winter months. Many of the stories they shared spoke of how all things in nature were related.

CUSTOMS

Festivals

The Nez Perce hold festivals several times a year to celebrate their heritage. During these events, tribe members drum, sing, and share traditional foods. Feasts are held to mark the arrival of edible plants and the beginning of major salmon runs.

A Nez Perce elder beats on a powwow drum.

Finding a guardian spirit

An important tradition for a Nez Perce child was to find his or her personal guardian spirit, known as the wyakin. Between the ages of 9 and 13, boys and girls were taught by an older tribe member who had a very strong wyakin. After they were taught for several years, the boy or girl went on a journey alone to find this personal spirit-helper. The child was not allowed to take food, water, or weapons on the trip. Sometimes, the wyakin came to the young person through dreams. At times, the young person went home, scared or homesick, even if he or she had not found the wyakin. In winter, young people who had been able to find the wyakin danced and sang. This helped them become one with their guardian spirits. As they watched and took part, other members of the tribe could often learn the identity of the young people's wyakins. The ceremony sometimes had contests to see who had received the greatest powers from their wyakin.

Hunting and war rituals

When a young boy had his first successful hunt, or caught his first fish, a ceremony took place. In this ceremony, the meat or fish was served to the tribe's adult males. The Nez Perce believed that this ritual would make the young boy a good provider. A similar ceremony was held for girls. Women of the tribe would eat the first roots or berries that a girl had gathered.

To prepare for war, Nez Perce men stripped to their breechcloths and moccasins. They put brightly colored paint on their faces and bodies. Red paint was placed on the part in a warrior's hair and across his forehead. Other colors were applied to his body in special patterns. The warriors also decorated themselves with animal feathers, fur, teeth, and claws. These ornaments represented the men's connection to their guardian spirits.

Current tribal issues

Modern Nez Perce have been involved in several legal cases. In some instances, their rights to hunt and fish on their homelands have been restored.

To prepare for battle, warriors painted their faces and wore elaborate costumes.

The Nez Perce people have also taken steps to remember their unique and tragic history. In 1996, descendants of the Wallowa band held their 20th annual ceremony to remember the people of

In Nez Perce tradition, a riderless horse represents tribe members who were killed in battle.

the tribe who died during the Nez Perce War of 1877. They gathered to smoke pipes, sing, and pray. They also held an empty saddle ceremony—in which horses are led without riders—in order to appease the spirits of the dead.

In the mid-1990s, declines in the timber and cattle markets brought hard economic times to non-native residents of Wallowa Valley. The residents then invited the Nez Perce to return to the area. A boom in tourism followed. The Nee-Me-Poo Trail, the Nez Perce National Historical Park, and the burial site of Old Chief Joseph have become major tourist sites. Valley residents raised money to build a visitor center and buy 160 acres of land for the tribe to use for cultural events.

Notable people

Chief Joseph (1840-1904), the son of Old Chief Joseph (died 1871), became leader of the tribe after his father's death. When the U.S. army attacked the Nez Perce as they fled to avoid a move to a reservation, Chief Joseph led his followers at the Battle of White Bird Canyon. His forces defeated the U.S. army, killed 33 soldiers, and suffered no casualties. They fought bravely and cleverly against U.S. forces until they were defeated four months later. Although his people were removed to sites in Washington and Idaho, Joseph was never allowed to return to his homeland. He died in 1904 before a Nez Perce reservation was set up there.

Members of the Nez Perce tribe celebrate a return to Wallowa Valley in 1997.

For More Information

Howard, Helen Addison. *Saga of Chief Joseph.* Lincoln: University of Nebraska Press, 1978.

Howes, Kathi. *The Nez Perce.* Vero Beach, FL: Rourke Publications, Inc., 1990.

Sneve, Virginia Driving Hawk. The Nez Perce. New York: Holiday House, 1994.

Trafzer, Clifford E. *The Nez Perce.* New York: Chelsea House, 1992.

Nez Perce Information and Education www.nezperce.com

Glossary

Adorned decorated with

Descendant relative of

Reservation land set aside and given to Native Americans

Ritual something that is a custom or done in a certain way

Sacred highly valued and important

Shaman a priest or priestess who uses magic for the purpose of curing the sick, divining the hidden, and controlling events

Tradition a custom or an established pattern of behavior

Treaty agreement

Tribe a group of people who live together in a community

Index